# TUTORING
A Guide for Success

**TITLES IN THE TUTORING SERIES**

**by Patricia S. Koskinen and Robert M. Wilson**

*Developing a Successful Tutoring Program* (for teachers and school administrators)

*Tutoring: A Guide for Success* (for adult tutors)

*A Guide for Student Tutors*

# TUTORING
## A Guide for Success

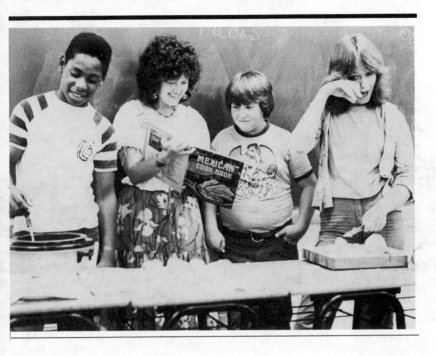

Patricia S. Koskinen and Robert M. Wilson

*Reading Center, College of Education*
*University of Maryland at College Park*

Teachers College, Columbia University, New York and London  1982

Published by Teachers College Press, 1234 Amsterdam Avenue,
New York, N.Y. 10027

Library of Congress Cataloging in Publication Data

Koskinen, Patricia S., 1942–
  Tutoring: a guide for success.

  (Tutoring series)
  Includes index.
  1.  Tutors and tutoring.  I.  Wilson, Robert Mills.
II.  Title.  III.  Series: Koskinen, Patricia S., 1942–
Tutoring series.
LC41.K675      371.3'94     81-18333
                        AACR2

ISBN 0-8077-2683-4

Manufactured in the United States of America

87   86   85   84   83   82      1  2  3  4  5  6

# Contents

# Preface

This book is designed to assist adults who want to tutor in schools. In it you will find practical suggestions to help make tutoring an enjoyable, successful experience. These ideas will get you off to a good start and help you think about the various aspects of tutoring.

Tutoring programs differ in many ways depending on the needs of particular students. As you use this book, you will want to adapt our suggestions to the unique needs of your students. You will find, however, that some ideas, such as those in chapter 4, will work well for you in almost any tutoring situation.

As you enter the tutoring activity, keep this book handy. You'll find it a convenient reference.

We wish you the very best. By becoming involved in tutoring you are providing a type of help that some students desperately need. We hope you enjoy the experience.

College Park, Md., 1982                                         P.S.K.
                                                                R.M.W.

# Acknowledgments

The pleasure of writing these books in the tutoring series was enhanced by the many people who contributed their ideas, suggestions, and enthusiastic support. Special appreciation is extended to the many coordinators of tutoring programs and tutors and their students whose excitement about their work stimulated us to write this book.

We are particularly grateful to John Koskinen who has been a skillful editor as well as a continuous source of encouragement. Marti King's reactions to the initial draft of our first manuscript were also especially helpful. We are indebted to Darryl Henry and Sandra Weiswasser for the warm, loving pictures they took of tutors and their students.

Other friends have also given generously of their time and expertise. Susan Coles and Sharon Villa provided not only expert typing but continuous patience and good cheer. Thomas Higgs contributed a number of creative illustrations for the text. Finally we appreciate the help of Lois Patton, Louise Craft, and Abby Levine, our editors, who have given us excellent advice and guided the final development of these books.

# **1** Introduction

## WHY ARE TUTORS IMPORTANT?

Some students need more individual attention than most teachers can offer. These students tend to misunderstand assignments, allow their attention to wander, disrupt the work of others, and miss opportunities to learn. One solution to this problem is to provide such students with tutors. When students know that someone cares and that individual attention is being provided, their academic performance often improves.

Some students need more attention because of excessive illness and absence from school. While it is very difficult for teachers to take the time needed to help these students catch up, it is a relatively easy task for a tutor who has only that objective in mind.

Other students need more attention because for some reason they have missed the mastery of a subskill and are, as a result, not able to profit from instruction. Teachers are usually aware of such problems but often cannot find enough time for makeup instruction. A tutor can provide that time. As the student regains confidence, normal instruction becomes effective.

Students receiving tutoring help are not the only ones who profit. Classmates benefit as otherwise distracted students begin to focus on learning. Teachers gain as the students become successful learners. Parents profit as they see their children happy and successful instead of sad and frustrated. The school population benefits by seeing a tutoring program as a helping program in which learning is important.

## WHAT ARE THE GOALS OF TUTORING?

Most tutoring programs have two major goals. They are:

- to help the students with their learning
- to help students feel good about themselves as learners

Other goals might be established for specific programs. These include:

- providing an experience otherwise not available to the students, such as instruction in English for a student who speaks only a foreign language.
- providing enrichment activities. For example, a photographer might give lessons on good picture-taking, or a person who has just returned from Mexico might enliven a unit of study on that country.
- assisting the teacher in the classroom. For example, a teacher might be tape-recording a student reading a story. A tutor might supervise the recording, permitting the teacher to attend to other instructional activities.

## WHO ARE SUCCESSFUL TUTORS?

People of many different ages and backgrounds have been successful tutors. Parents of school-age children, retired citizens, and other adults from the community constitute a source of tutors. Students from the upper elementary grades through college have also been willing and effective tutors. Age and background are not as important as the interest and personal qualities of the tutor.

The following characteristics have been repeatedly mentioned as important qualities of successful tutors. How many boxes can you check?

Check
here

1. Are you reliable and dependable? ☐
   (Tutors come to tutoring regularly and
   on time.)
2. Do you help others feel good about them- ☐
   selves? (Tutors accept students as they
   are, are patient, and give lots of friendly
   support.)
3. Do you respect confidential information? ☐
   (Tutors keep information about students
   and the school confidential.)
4. Are you flexible? (Tutors adjust to school ☐
   changes.)
5. Are you regularly prepared for activities? ☐
   (Tutors plan for the sessions and find
   material that reflects the students' interests.)
6. Do you respect the rights of others? ☐
   (Tutors support teachers' individual
   ways of working.)

If you have most of these qualities and are willing to spend time helping another person, then you have the potential to be an effective tutor.

# 2 Getting to Know Your Tutoring Program

EACH tutoring program is different, and you will want to know the specific procedures of your program. You'll need to find out who, when, and where you will be tutoring.

## WHO AM I GOING TO TUTOR?

There are many ways tutors and students get together. Often programs pair tutors and students by the times that are mutually convenient. Sometimes it is possible to work with students of a particular age, sex, or personality type or with those having special interests. If you have a strong preference for the type of student you would like to work with, let your tutoring coordinator know. Sometimes special arrangements can be made. If you want to tutor in a specific subject area or have interests you want to share, you should also mention this to your coordinator.

## WHAT WILL I BE DOING DURING THE TUTORING SESSION?

Tutoring can be done in most subject areas using a variety of methods and materials. Excellent programs have been developed, for example, in reading, mathematics, science, art, and athletics. In many programs tutors make their own teaching materials, while in others a tutor might be given programmed materials and asked to follow them exactly. Your students' teachers will identify the content of tutoring and decide on the procedures you are to use.

You will receive training to help you understand the content of tutoring as well as how to make the topic meaningful to your students. The type and amount of training will depend upon what you will be doing. Generally there will be initial training sessions to orient you to the program. These give you information about your tutoring situation and details of how to work with students. There may also be specific times that tutors are asked to get together after they have been working for a while. These ongoing training sessions are important because they allow tutors to share ideas and to learn new teaching techniques.

## WHEN AM I GOING TO TUTOR?

It is important to pick tutoring times that are convenient for you. These should be times when you can work regularly. Once these times have been established, both your students and their teachers will be relying on you. They will arrange their schedules so your students will be free to meet with you.

As a reminder, you might want to make a schedule such as the one in figure 1, so your students will know when to go for

**FIGURE 1**   Tutoring Schedule

---

Student ___*Ron Weaver*___

| Day | Time | Place |
|-----|------|-------|
| Monday | 1:15–1:45 | Cafeteria |
| Thursday | 2:00–2:30 | Music room |

*Henry Black*
Tutor

---

tutoring. If for some reason your tutoring time is no longer convenient, tell the coordinator, who will try to make a change. After a tutoring time is established, it should be regularly reconfirmed. Check with the students at the end of each session to see if any special events are to take place during your next scheduled time. Encourage the students to take responsibility for informing you when they will not be available for tutoring. If your students are frequently unable to come, check with the coordinator to see if a change can be made.

## WHERE AM I GOING TO TUTOR?

Finding a place for tutoring is always a challenge in a busy school. Tutors have successfully worked with students in the corner of a classroom, in the library, or in just about any place where space is available. If you have more than one place for tutoring, be sure to help your students understand where they will meet you. When you are working with a young child, you may need to pick up your student from the classroom until the child becomes familiar with the tutoring times and places.

## WHAT DO I DO WHEN I CAN'T GO TO TUTORING?

Your students will be looking forward to your tutoring sessions just as much as you. Since they will be disappointed when you can't come, be sure to let them know in advance. If you cannot meet with your students, you also need to tell the coordinator or teachers.

It may also be appropriate to write a note to your students' teachers. If you will be away for an extended period, the coordinator may be able to find a substitute until you return. Find out the specific procedures that your program uses. Be sure to have the telephone numbers of people to call.

## WHERE DO I GO FOR MORE INFORMATION ABOUT TUTORING?

If you have a question, *no matter how small,* get an answer to it. People in the tutoring program want to help you get settled and feel comfortable. You need to find out the names and telephone numbers of people to contact when you need help. Also find out what times they are free to talk with you.

Many schools have a tutoring information center where they post notices for tutors about meetings and schedule changes. Find out where you can get information about assembly dates, class trips, and other activities that might interfere with your tutoring time.

# 3 Getting Started

## GENERAL SCHOOL PROCEDURES

As you prepare for your tutoring session, you need to become familiar with the school in which you will be working. You will slowly get to know the people in the school and the community resources, but there are some essential school procedures that you should be aware of from the very beginning.

Every school has a number of rules or guidelines for people who work there. Check your school's procedures with your coordinator. Schools may have guidelines for the following areas:

*Fire Emergency.* Check on safe exit areas.

*Health Emergencies.* Find out if there is a nurse or health aide in the building. The school principal, teacher, or secretary should be told immediately when someone is hurt or sick.

*Use of School Materials and Equipment.* Schools generally have limited supplies, but some may be available for your use. You should find out if someone is in charge of supplies and when you can use them. If you need a piece of equipment, see if you can be trained to use it. You generally must sign up to use all school materials.

*Parking.* Be sure to find out where it is permissible to park.

*Dress Code.* Since you are in a responsible role as a tutor, you need to find out what type of clothing is allowed in the school. For example, sometimes teachers and tutors are asked *not* to wear jeans.

*Trips.* Students need parental permission to leave the school building. If you want to take a student on a trip, check with your coordinator ahead of time to find out what you will need to do. Generally a note is written to the parents explaining the purpose of the trip and requesting their signatures.

*Confidentiality.* During your work you may find out personal information about your students. Their academic abilities or personal lives need to be kept private.

## DEVELOPING A SUPPORTIVE RELATIONSHIP

People learn when they feel comfortable and secure. One of your major roles as a tutor is to provide support for your students and to be someone they can trust and respect. When they feel comfortable being with you, they will begin to ask you questions, listen to your answers, and try to learn.

One way to begin a relationship is to talk with your students about their interests. In preparation for your first meeting, develop a list of questions you might ask. These questions can relate to such things as favorite TV shows, music, hobbies, or pets. Figure 2 contains a list of questions tutors developed to help them get to know their students. These tutors picked about four questions to ask during the first session and saved the others for future meetings. When selecting the questions you are going to ask, try to find ones that will help your students feel good about themselves and the tutoring session.

Because your students will be curious about you, be prepared to share something about yourself at the first session. Bring in something that is of interest to you and might be of interest to them. Tutors have shared such things as a photograph of a pet, a stamp collection, or a favorite baseball. This mutual sharing can mark the beginning of a relationship. If a small part of each tutoring session is devoted to talking about personal interests, you will continue to learn new things about your students and further develop your friendship.

**FIGURE 2**   Student Interest Inventory

1.   Do you like films or TV? What do you like to watch?
2.   What kinds of sports do you like to play?
3.   Do you like animals? What kinds?
4.   What kinds of books or magazines do you like to read?
5.   What do you want to be when you grow up?
6.   Do you have any brothers or sisters?
7.   What do you like to do in your spare time?
8.   What do you like about school? What don't you like about school?
9.   What is your favorite musical group?

## PLANNING YOUR TUTORING SESSIONS

Careful planning is essential for successful tutoring. While preparation for tutoring takes less time when you become familiar with the situation, even experienced tutors still allow time for planning before each session. You will need to familiarize yourself with the materials given to you or make your own materials directed toward your students' interests. You also will need to consider how to best present material to your students. Find out how much time you have for each session and be sure to stick within that time frame. Each session should include at least the following elements:

- helping the students feel at ease
- working with a specific skill activity
- discussing students' reactions to the activity
- making plans for the next session

To help students feel at ease, call them by name, smile, and show that you're happy to see them. Any of the interests you have discovered in your first tutoring session can be used as conversation starters. Let your students know that you like them and that they are going to have a good time learning and working with you.

After your students are feeling welcome and comfortable, briefly review what you did at your last session. This activity will help jog their memories and start them thinking about the skills being developed during tutoring.

When planning your skill activities, find ways to make them meaningful to the students. Whenever possible include opportunities for students to discuss, read, write, and manipulate objects. Pictures and concrete objects also greatly facilitate learning for students of all ages. Try to include opportunities for students to make choices. You might bring in three activities and let them decide which should be done during the session. At other times you might discuss the activities for the session and let the students decide which should be done first.

Determining how much work to give students comes with careful observation of their strengths and needs. Since one of your major goals for tutoring is to help your students enjoy learning, you'll want to be sure they can successfully do the activities you have prepared. Watch the pacing of your activities. As you notice students learning easily, go on to the next level of difficulty. When an activity appears to be causing confusion, slow down and try to determine the exact area of difficulty. There is a fine line between challenging students and frustrating them. Tutoring should be a time for students to succeed, so if there is a question as to the difficulty of an activity, be sure that students find success.

Since it is sometimes hard to judge how much work to prepare for each session, always have an extra activity. This activity
can be used if your students finish all the things you have
planned, or if one of your activities turns out to be inappropri-
ate. Be sure you bring this activity to every tutoring session
because you'll never know when you'll need it. The following are
a few activities that have been successfully used by tutors:

1.   Share a book with your students. It might be a book with
     lots of facts such as the *Guinness Book of World Records,*
     one with simple projects to make, or just an interesting
     story.
2.   Read and discuss a newspaper or magazine article on a
     current topic of interest.
3.   Play a word game such as hangman or do a crossword
     puzzle.
4.   Discuss a recent activity in which students have partici-
     pated. Take dictation and have the students read it with
     you.
5.   Take turns reading each other jokes or riddles.

Whenever possible, choose an activity that is related in some way
to the subject matter of the tutoring.

The final segment of the lesson should involve the students
in evaluation and planning. Find out what they felt they learned
by doing the activity and what they would like to do the next
time. Some tutors also save a short, particularly high interest
activity (such as a game or jokes) for the last part of the session.
This assures that students leave with a desire to return again
soon.

In your role as tutor you will be spending a lot of time asking
questions, listening to responses, and then reacting to these
responses. It is extremely important that you plan ways to give
positive, friendly support in each of these situations. Be sure
your questions are clearly stated and generally require more
than just a "yes" or "no" answer. Show that you are interested in
your students by carefully listening to them. Praise their work.
Instead of being impatient when your students do not do something you expect them to do, find ways of emphasizing the
positive aspects of their answers. Your patience, sense of humor,

and praise will be rewarded with student enthusiasm and self-confidence.

## RECORD-KEEPING

Record-keeping is an extremely important part of successful tutoring. Even the most experienced teachers forget the details of some activities unless they take notes. By keeping a record of what happens at each session, you will be able to review what you have done, follow up on successful ideas, and adapt lessons as a result of previous experiences.

There are many ways to keep records. You need to find a format that you like. A page from a log used by one group of tutors is shown in figure 3. The first part of the form was

**FIGURE 3**   Tutoring Log

Name_ *Anita* _____   Date *March 4* _____

*Plans*

1.   Help student feel at ease.

2.   Activity_ " *Bingo game with 20 words. Copying new words to make the "fish" game.* "

3.   Other activities (planned or unplanned)_ *Reading Frog and Toad Together.* _____

*Comments on Tutoring Session* (things that happened, successes, problems, ideas for future sessions)

*Anita really enjoys playing board games. She knows 12 words well. She asked to play "Candy Land" with more words next time. She didn't want to read the book, so I read 4 pages and she read one.*

How do you feel about your tutoring session?

*Anita was tired but perked up with "Bingo". The session was better than last time.*

**FIGURE 4**   Notes from a Tutoring Log

Name: *John*

| Date | Topic | Comments |
|------|-------|----------|
| Feb. 6 | Review 5 and 6 multiplication tables. Use flash cards with football games. | Knew most of the 5 tables. Needs a review of 6×6, 7, 8, 9. Loves the games — wants more sports games with basketball and soccer. |
| Feb. 9 | Review a few 5 problems as an encouraging warm-up; then play a basketball game with 6 and 7 tables. | Still needs work with the late 6 tables. Need to use some counting beans in the near future. |

completed before the session; the rest, afterwards. The log served both as the tutor's planning book and as an evaluation form. Another type of record-keeping format is shown in figure 4. This type of reporting can be as brief or complete as you desire. It will often contain pertinent evaluation information to be used in planning. As can be seen in figure 4, the tutor who wrote these notes planned the lesson for February 9 as a result of information from the previous lesson. Regardless of the type of record-keeping you use, daily plans must be kept. In this way you can evaluate the work that has been done, and both you and your students can clearly see how much has been accomplished. Check with your coordinator to see if your school has a recommended record-keeping system.

## CHECKLIST FOR THE FIRST DAY OF TUTORING

As you plan for your first meetings with your students, you may want to write down all the necessary information. Use the checklist in figure 5 to help organize your planning.

**FIGURE 5**  Checklist for the First Day of Tutoring

---

Do you have the following information?                    Check the
                                                          box when
                                                          you have the
                                                          information

1. _____     ☐
                    Student's name

2. _____     ☐
                 Day and time of tutoring

3. _____     ☐
                   Place of tutoring

4. _____     ☐
                 Place to pick up student

5. Plans for tutoring

   List of get-acquainted questions            ☐
   High interest activity                      ☐
   An extra activity                           ☐

6. _____     _____
        School contact person          Telephone

7. General school procedures

   Fire emergency_____   ☐

   Health emergency_____   ☐

   Dress code_____   ☐

   Parking_____   ☐

---

# 4 Tutoring Strategies That Make a Difference

THIS section focuses on general teaching strategies that are needed for most types of tutoring. Many of these strategies were briefly mentioned in chapter 3 because they are so important for successful tutoring. If you are interested in an explanation of these strategies and ideas for implementing them, read through this chapter. Look at your teaching to see which of these ideas you are already using and then slowly try to incorporate more of them into your teaching.

## FOCUSING ON STRENGTHS

*Objective.* To help students feel good about themselves as able learners.

*Explanation.* Many students who need the help of a tutor do not feel good about themselves. They do not feel that they can learn things easily. Sometimes this perception is the result of the group instruction that teachers must use. The pace of the instruction leaves certain students behind, and they get poor grades on papers and report cards. By focusing on strengths, tutors can change those negative feelings to positive ones. The following suggestions are examples of ways a tutor can focus on strengths.

*Suggestions*
1. Mark correct answers on student papers—not incorrect ones.
2. When grading a paper, indicate the number correct, not the number wrong.
3. Write personal notes to your students about observed behavior that you would like to reinforce.
4. When the students do well, write notes to their teachers and parents.
5. Create an award letter that indicates the successful completion of a contract, project or assignment. For example, see figure 6.
6. Develop progress charts that indicate the number of successes—words learned, assignments completed, questions answered. For example, see figure 7.

## WORKING WITH STUDENT INTERESTS

*Objective.* To make tutoring sessions interesting for the students.

*Explanation.* Some students find much of what goes on in school to be boring. As a tutor you have a chance to change that.

**FIGURE 6** Student Award

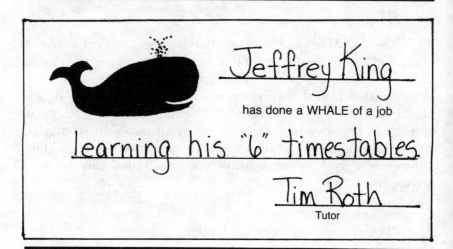

**FIGURE 7** Progress Chart

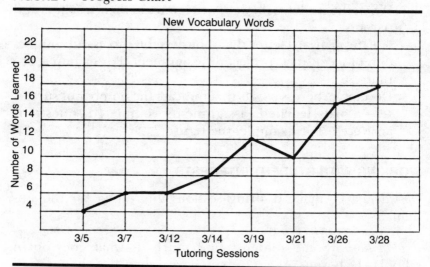

If you can make lessons interesting, you will have attentive, interested students with whom to work.

*Suggestions*
1.  Determine things that interest your students. Ask about interests in sports, TV, books, and other things. Make note of these interests immediately after your sessions so that you will remember them.
2.  Plan to use something from the list of interests in as many lessons as possible. For example, if a student likes dogs, plan to read a story about dogs or collect some dog pictures from magazines and share them.
3.  Watch for changing interests. Sports interests, for example, can change when a season is over. It is important not to overdo an emphasis on a given interest. By paying attention to your students' responses, you can usually tell when an interest is declining.
4.  Talk with your students' teachers about what you are doing in this area. Teachers usually have good ideas about how to utilize a student's interests.


## LISTENING TO STUDENTS

*Objective.*   To let students know you are interested in what they have to say.

*Explanation.*   What students say is important to them. Many students report that they do not feel that their teachers listen to them. When that feeling persists, communication is hampered. Students begin to feel that what they say is not valued.

*Suggestions*
1.  Be certain to look at your students when they are talking to you.
2.  Use your body to show you are listening carefully. At times you might nod your head in agreement, smile, gesture with

your hands, or lean forward with your body to indicate your sincere interest.

3.  Try to understand the full intent of the message being sent to you. At times the words will suggest meanings that cannot be stated. For example, a student might be saying, "I need your help" but might be feeling, "I'm dumb."

4.  Hear students out. At times adults interrupt them before they have completed their thoughts. Such interruptions indicate that their ideas are not valued.

## RESPONDING TO YOUR STUDENTS

*Objective.*   To encourage students and help them feel accepted by the way you respond to them.

*Explanation.*   Each time we respond to something that students say or do, we are giving them information about our feelings. It is important to know what you are communicating when you respond to students.

*Suggestions*
1.  It helps to provide encouragement when things are not going well. Comments such as "Let's try that again. I'll help you" tend to make students feel like persevering.

2.  When their achievements are recognized, students can be encouraged to continue trying. For example, acknowledge the eight words spelled correctly instead of the two that are missed. Of course you will need to deal with the two mis-spellings, but only after you recognize the correctly spelled words.

3.  Attempt to keep eye contact. Eye contact is one way to promote sincerity as you respond to your students.

4.  Try to respond without being evaluative. Discussion and disagreement need not be conducted in terms that make the students feel "wrong."

5.  Think of different ways to tell your students they have done a good job. Try comments such as:
    •  What a great answer!
    •  Excellent! That was a difficult problem!

- You really remembered a lot!
- Good thinking!
- I like the way you did that!
6. Try to communicate by your responses that you enjoy working with your students. Smiles, nods, and pleasant voice tones all indicate your enjoyment.

## HELPING STUDENTS PAY ATTENTION

*Objective.* To assist students in concentrating on their learning activities.

*Explanation.* Most of the activities involving learning require students to concentrate thoroughly. We call this *attention to task.* We have all experienced difficulty concentrating on a task, and we realize that we have not learned what we set out to do. Tutors can try some activities to help their students attend to the tasks they have planned.

*Suggestions*
1. Plan activities for short periods of time. Working with sight vocabulary for half an hour would be boring for most students. A ten-minute lesson might not be.
2. Share your time plan with your students. If a part of a session is to be for ten minutes, then tell them. Many students will react favorably when they know that attention to a given task is expected for a short period of time.
3. Make certain that students know when they are finished. Some students view school as a never-ending series of activities. Set up your activities so that students will know what must be done to complete the task.
4. Let students know that you care about their attention to task. Send a note to their teachers when it has been good.
5. Have your students self-evaluate their attention to task. They might be given a rating sheet, and they can circle how well they did. For example, Today, I worked:
   - very well
   - well
   - not too well

If they self-evaluate "well" or "not too well," then you can ask them why. Many times they will explain their lack of attention to task in such a way that you can make adjustments. Students appreciate such adjustments. It shows them that you care about them as learners.

## HELPING STUDENTS COMPLETE ASSIGNMENTS INDEPENDENTLY

*Objective.*    To prepare students to complete assignments independently.

*Explanation.*    Many students work well under teacher direction but find it difficult to complete assignments on their own. It is common for students to ask their tutors for help with assignments.

*Suggestions*
1.    When students ask for help, first try to determine ways in which they might help themselves. For example, if they ask for the spelling of a word, suggest that they use a dictionary or try to spell it on their own. Independence is the final objective.
2.    Help students see when their assignments are completed. Set some goals that can be achieved. If the assignment is lengthy, set goals for sections of it.
3.    Help develop the habit of checking assignments before turning them in to the teacher. Again, set goals for self-checking. For example, students might ask themselves the following questions:
     • Are words spelled correctly?
     • Is the assignment neat in appearance?
     • Is the assignment complete?
4.    Help students use resources within the school. For example, go with them to the library and show how useful the card catalog can be.
5.    Once you have helped a student with an assignment, try to obtain feedback from the teacher. Determine if your effort was helpful and if you need to help in other ways.

## CREATING A CHALLENGE

*Objective.*    To make learning enjoyable and profitable.

*Explanation.*    When learning occurs because of student effort, we call that challenge. When a student need not make an effort, we call that boredom. When a student makes an effort and fails, we call that frustration. A challenging learning climate is the desirable one.

*Suggestions*
1.  Try to set goals for each lesson that you believe are within the grasp of your students if they make an effort.
2.  When you notice that your students can succeed without effort and that their attention seems to drift away, change the activity or step up the tempo.
3.  When you notice that your students are weary and unsuccessful, change the activity or slow the tempo.
4.  When you begin a new type of activity, make it last only a short time. For example, tell your students that you will be working with them on an activity for ten minutes. At the end of that time determine if they want to do more or want a change.
5.  Make certain that your students know when they have been successful. Illustrate their successes in a variety of ways. Have them self-evaluate. If they do not believe they have done well when they have, then discuss the goals and the resulting behaviors that were successful.

## ENCOURAGING RISK-TAKING

*Objective.*    To encourage your students to try, even when the task is difficult.

*Explanation.*    Learning involves a certain amount of risk-taking. If people try and are wrong, then learning can become very unpleasant. If people do not try, then they cannot be wrong, but they won't learn either. Tutors can make adjustments that will enhance risk-taking.

*Suggestions.*    Many of the suggestions presented in this chapter encourage risk-taking. Focusing on strengths, asking personal questions, and attending to student interests are just a few of the ideas that are discussed.

Here are a few additional suggestions:

1.  Plan seating arrangements that make it seem that you are a helper instead of a threat. Sitting beside a student instead of across a desk is one helpful seating adjustment.
2.  Encourage students to work in pairs when it is appropriate. Pairing encourages risk-taking because the students work out their responses before sharing them with the teacher or tutor. For example, students can work together making reports, checking their arithmetic, or preparing oral reading.
3.  Plan a system for communicating with your students. You might develop a place where notes can be dropped off and picked up. Helping students evaluate their performance also enhances communication (see "Helping Students Pay Attention" earlier in this chapter).

## QUESTIONING STRATEGIES

*Objective.*    To help students respond during questioning.

*Explanation.*    Sometimes students are afraid to respond to questions. They may have been embarrassed in the past when they came up with incorrect answers. Tutors must make plans for questioning that will encourage students to respond fully, without fear of embarrassment. The following suggestions show ways tutors can use questioning effectively.

*Suggestions*
1.  Allow time for students to prepare answers. Tutors sometimes expect immediate responses and interrupt the thought process with more questions.
2.  Prepare questions that are personal. Personal questions are those that have no "right" answers. For example:

- What did you like best about that story?
- What part of the story was most interesting to you?
- Tell me what you think was the most important event in that story.

3.  Create a discussion atmosphere. Instead of a series of unrelated questions, share your feelings about the story. The purpose of questioning is to develop a thorough understanding of what has been read. Have your students develop their own questions to ask you. Being able to create a question requires careful thought.

4.  Prepare questions that encourage thinking. Many tutors fall into the trap of asking questions that require students to recall facts. For example, "Who was the other girl in this story?" "What was the dog's name?" Instead, ask questions that let students think carefully about the story and require more than a one-word answer. For example: "Why do you think Margi liked her dog so much?" "Who did you think did the right thing with his dog?" "Why?"

5.  Allow for different ways of answering questions. Some students would rather reply orally, while others might prefer to write their answers. Some students like to answer into a tape recorder. Search for ways to make your students comfortable when responding to questions.


## DEVELOPING A COMFORTABLE LEARNING ENVIRONMENT

*Objective.*   To place the student in a comfortable learning situation.

*Explanation.*   Learning can be enhanced when the environment is comfortable. If it is too hot, too cold, or too stuffy, then it is difficult for students to enjoy the learning activity. This is true even when the activity is well-planned and interesting. Tutors do not always have control over all features of the learning environment, but they should attempt to make adjustments when they are needed.

*Suggestions*
1.  Do little things to make the area pleasant. A poster or some pictures can help to make a drab area inviting. A smiley face on the chalkboard can be effective.
2.  Pay attention to the temperature. If you are in a room that is too hot or too cold, try to make a change. If you cannot, adapt to the situation. When it is too cold, be certain to plan some physical activities between parts of your session. If it too hot, try to keep physical activities to a minimum.
3.  Try to be sure that your area has good ventilation. Open a window, or get near a door or ventilation fan. If you cannot do this, ask your contact person for help.
4.  Watch out for distracting noise. If you are next door to the music room, gymnasium, or other noise-producing places, learning might be very difficult. Ask for a different area for tutoring if noise becomes a problem.
5.  Be sure that chairs and desks are the appropriate size for your students. If they are not, ask for them to be changed.
6.  Try to make the area personally meaningful for your students. Perhaps you can have some of their past good work available for them to see. A personal photograph, a poster, or artwork might have appeal for some students.

# 5 Getting to Know Your School

## MEETING THE SCHOOL STAFF

While the principal is usually in charge of a school, many other people play prominent roles. Classroom teachers and resource specialists are leaders in the area of instruction. Staff such as the school secretary, custodian, and lunchroom workers not only help in the management of the school but support students in unique and important ways. Most staff are willing to help when they feel they are respected and accepted. Be sensitive to the feelings of others, and you will find yourself becoming a valued member of the school community.

## LEARNING ABOUT YOUR SCHOOL'S INSTRUCTIONAL PROGRAM

To help you understand how your tutoring fits into the total instructional program, try to get an overview of the present school program. Find out what subjects your students are studying and whether they are receiving other special services. Your coordinator will be able to find out this information for you.

It can also be helpful to learn what resources are available for tutors to use. In addition to the coordinator, the school's media specialist (librarian) and special subject teachers may be of assistance. School personnel will be most helpful if you make an appointment at a time that is convenient for them.

## FINDING OUT ABOUT THE SCHOOL'S MANAGEMENT PROCEDURES

Most schools have many operational procedures. It is important for you to become aware of these procedures as they relate to students and to teachers and other staff. In addition to regulations for events such as fire and health emergencies, you need to become familiar with additional procedures that help in the smooth operation of the school. For example, there are guidelines for the use of the playground, lunchroom, and media center.

Of particular interest to you may be the general rules for student behavior. Learn these school rules and try to support them as best you can. For example, if walking rather than running in the halls is encouraged, or if using soft voices rather than yelling is requested, have your students follow these rules. Students are aware of many of the school rules but may not always follow them. Your guidance is important to help maintain the normal routine. Be sure to ask your coordinator if you have questions relating to your role in complying with the school rules.

## WORKING WITH YOUR STUDENTS' TEACHERS

You will probably have a variety of opportunities to talk with your students' teachers. While they support your tutoring (they wouldn't allow students to be tutored during instructional time if they didn't), they may be very busy and have difficulty finding adequate time to talk with you. Check with your coordinator or your students' teachers about setting a time to talk about your students' progress. When talking with the teacher, use a positive and friendly manner. If you are frustrated or concerned about your work with a student, try not to appear as if you are blaming the teacher. Teachers are very willing to help if they feel your support rather than your criticism.

Teachers will also appreciate your showing respect for the students' instructional time. You can do this by:

- coming to tutoring regularly and on time
- being sure the students are back in class on time
- notifying the teachers when you will not be coming to tutor so plans can be made for the students
- being flexible so a student can participate in a special class activity that unexpectedly comes up at the regular tutoring time

## GETTING TO KNOW THE SCHOOL'S COMMUNITY

If you are not already familiar with the community in which you are working, you will find getting to know it both interesting and useful. Since your students may live in the area, knowledge of who lives in the community, what stores are there, and the recreational opportunities available will give you information to share with them. By knowing about community resources such as the library or after-school programs, you may also be able to recommend activities to your students. Once you are familiar with the community, you will not only understand your students better but you will begin to feel comfortable in the area and will look forward to working with students there.

# 6 Keeping Up Student Interest

NOW that you have begun tutoring, you may be feeling more comfortable in your work. Because your students will be changing and developing, you need to be flexible. Tutoring also requires creative energy and attention: You must be able to meet the needs of your students and maintain their enthusiasm about learning.

## EVALUATE THE TUTORING SESSIONS

Even though you only work with students for a short time each week, you will be able to develop a relationship that encourages learning. To do this, however, you will need to evaluate your tutoring sessions, continually looking for things that are going well and areas where change needs to take place. When thinking about each session, you might ask yourself the following kinds of questions:

*Did I Come on Time and Was I Prepared?*   Students know whether their tutoring is an exciting productive time or whether it is just a chance to get out of class and fool around. One way to show that you respect the students is to prepare for your sessions and come when you are expected.

*Did I Show a Personal Interest in the Students?*   Spending just a few minutes talking to the students about their interests, apart from the tutoring topic, can show you care about them as people.

*Did I Develop Meaningful Activities That Were of Interest to the Students?*   Check your activities to see if:

- Students know why they are doing an activity.
- Materials are directed toward your students' interests.
- Students have some choice about the work they are doing.
- Students can succeed if they try.

*Did I Provide Time for Students to Discuss Their Reactions to the Activities?*   Letting students evaluate an activity both involves them in reflecting on their work and can give you ideas for planning future sessions.

*Were Students Aware of the Things They Did Well?*   Help your students understand all the ways they are progressing. Celebrate the small steps that indicate progress as well as the big ones. In addition to the praise you give them, be sure to help students discover their own successes.

*Did I Know the School Rules and Routines?*   By knowing the school rules, you will know what kind of behavior to expect. This knowledge will help you to encourage responsible student conduct.

## CELEBRATE PARTICIPATION IN TUTORING

Students enjoy being recognized for their involvement in tutoring. Participation awards such as the one in figure 8 have been highly valued by students. Tutors have also planned special activities such as picnics, treasure hunts, pizza parties, or trips for their students. These are just a few ways of showing your appreciation for their hard work.

**FIGURE 8**   Student Award

**GREAT JOB AWARD**
**for**

_Cheryl Kennedy_

# 7 Keeping Up Your Own Interest

YOU are the key to successful tutoring. You need to feel comfortable working with students and to know that your time is being well-spent. As you continue tutoring and constantly revise your activities to meet the changing needs of your students, be sure you do things that also meet your own needs. The following ideas can help keep up your own enthusiasm:

*Ask Questions.* If you have a question or concern, talk with your coordinator. Getting a question answered, even a very small one, may prevent future problems. Some tutors keep a sheet called "Questions to Ask the Coordinator/Teacher." This helps them remember their ideas when they meet with the coordinator or teacher.

*Organize Your Tutoring Materials.*   Keep your materials for tutoring where you can easily locate them. Some tutors use a three-ring binder with pockets to store their daily plans, copies of school rules, and other items. When tutoring involves things such as games and books, tutors have found a sturdy bag efficiently keeps things together.

*Talk with Other Tutors.*   Since tutors do not usually work at the same time or may not meet regularly, you need to seek out other tutors. Share your experiences, and you may get many new ideas for working with students. At the same time, you will give and receive general support.

*Attend Tutor Meetings.*   Whenever possible, go to the meetings planned for tutors. These meetings can help solve common problems that tutors face and are a source of new teaching techniques.

*Look for Signs of Progress.*   Your tutoring experiences will vary from session to session. Even if you consistently plan well, your students may be very enthusiastic some days and rather tired or even irritable others. Be prepared for these variations. As you evaluate each of your sessions, don't be discouraged if there is an occasional "bad" day. Take note of your concerns but also be sure to observe the good things that happen. Look for small signs of progress or success such as:

- a student beginning to come to tutoring on time
- a student working on an assignment a few minutes longer than he or she was able to do before
- your developing an especially interesting activity
- your being more patient than usual
- your explaining something particularly well so that the student was able to understand it

These successes are signs of progress that should make you and your students feel proud. Take pleasure in finding things that have gone well. These small successes are what make tutoring worthwhile.

# 8 Common Problems

TUTORING involves problem-solving. Tutors and teachers always run into problems that need to be solved. Here are some questions frequently asked by tutors about common problems they have faced. Some suggestions for dealing with these problems are also given.

1. What do I do if a student does not want to try an activity?
   *Suggestions:*
   • Tell the student you know that it is difficult, but that you are there to help.
   • Urge the student to try, and explain that a mistake will not be counted against him or her.
   • Do the first part of the activity together as a team. Then let the student try it alone.

2.   What do I do if the student is bored?
     *Suggestions:*
     • Reexamine the activity to make certain it is appropriate.
     • Move the student into a decision-making role. For exam-
       ple, given three activities, which one would the student
       prefer?
     • Check to see if the student might be missing an exciting
       activity in the classroom. If so, suggest that the two of you
       return to participate.

3.   What do I do if a student fails to bring necessary materials to
     the tutoring session?
     *Suggestions:*
     • Have extra materials available.
     • Make a plan so that this is less likely to happen again. Try
       checking with the student before leaving the pickup area
       to make sure everything that is needed is on hand, or write
       a note together to remind the student to bring things for
       the next session.

4.   What do I do if a student breaks school rules?
     *Suggestions:*
     • Go over the rules to be certain that the student knows
       them.
     • Try to determine why the student broke the rules. Were
       there circumstances that would explain the behavior?
     • Seek the advice of the tutoring coordinator.

5.   What do I do if a student seems angry or upset a lot?
     *Suggestions:*
     If you have not been able to find out what the problem is by
     talking with the student, you might try the following ideas.
     • Be at the place of tutoring before the student so you can
       greet him or her and start immediately with a high interest
       activity. Some students have trouble with transitions and
       may become upset when working with a new person in a
       different setting. Help the student feel at ease and cared
       for as quickly as possible.
     • Develop activities that are fun and that frequently make
       the student feel successful. Your student may have been

failing in the classroom. This student may be afraid, angry, and embarrassed because another person is going to find out that he or she is a failure.

- Talk with the teacher about the specific behavior of the student. Ask how the student feels about going to tutoring, whether a favorite activity is being missed, or if the work load is overwhelming. If you suspect the student is upset because of a problem at home (for example, an alcoholic parent or abuse), tell the teacher the reasons for your concern. He or she will be able to give you some guidance for working with this student.

6.  What do I do if a student doesn't understand an activity?
    *Suggestions:*
    - Break the activity into small parts and let the student work on one part at a time.
    - Explain the activity using easier words and examples related to the student's life. Use pictures or concrete objects when appropriate.
    - Do the activity with the student, explaining each step as you progress. Let the student do the first part with you. Gradually let him or her do new steps independently while you complete and explain those that have not yet been mastered. Do this until the whole activity can be performed independently. At this point be sure you are available to give encouragement.

7.  What do I do if a student gives incorrect answers and I want to focus on student strengths?
    *Suggestions:*
    - Compliment good thinking and urge the student to focus on another possible solution.
    - Look for parts of the response that were correct.
    - Provide time for the student to rethink the response without any reaction from you.

# 9 Special Tutoring Situations

SOME tutoring situations require special skills and understanding. It is impossible to imagine what all of those situations would be. When you find unusual situations for which you are not prepared, you should contact the tutoring coordinator immediately.

In this section, four special situations will be addressed. They include:

- tutoring students with disabilities
- tutoring your own child
- tutoring more than one student
- team tutoring

## TUTORING STUDENTS WITH DISABILITIES

Today disabled students can be found in regular classrooms. They are likely candidates for tutoring. Tutors can play a vital role in the education of the disabled. You will need to know some of the following views about working with the disabled.

1.  Persons with disabilities are handicapped when the situation in which they must learn has not been or cannot be adjusted to the disability. If the system adjusts to the disability, then the person is not handicapped in that situation. For example, a ramp makes access to buildings possible for those confined to wheelchairs.
2.  Under the law students with disabilities are to learn in regular classrooms whenever feasible. In this way the disabled students can feel as normal as possible, and nondisabled students can realize the disabled are normal.
3.  Many teachers cannot provide the time and attention to work with disabled students. A tutor might be able to provide that time and attention.
4.  Tutors will need to call upon the resources within the school for assistance. The principal, resource teachers, special education teachers, reading specialists, classroom teachers, and librarians all might have help to offer.

## TUTORING YOUR OWN CHILD

At times tutors realize that their training and experiences might be used to instruct their own children in the home. If you decide to tutor your own children, consider the following:

1.  Regardless of your effectiveness as a tutor in a school, you might not be the right person to work with your own children in any structured type of way. The emotions involved with working with your children and the intense desire to see them be successful sometimes interfere with a good instructional relationship.
2.  There are, of course, many times when a parent is the only appropriate tutor in the home, and a parent can be quite helpful. A few guidelines might be of use:

- Keep tutoring activities pleasant. When things become unpleasant, stop or change the activity.
- Plan to work together for short periods. Try not to let your children feel trapped in a never-ending tutoring situation. Ten to fifteen minutes is the recommended maximum time, especially for very young children.
- Whenever possible, place your children in decision-making roles. Let them decide how much time and help they need, when and where to work, and many other things. Decision-making lets your children feel in some control of the situation.
- Focus on strengths. All children need to be seen as successful people in the eyes of their parents.
- Support your schools. At times parents who tutor their own children become frustrated and end up criticizing the school. The damaging effects of this upon children's attitudes toward school can be tremendous. If parents have concerns about home assignments, they might better contact the school than complain about the school to their children.
- Sometimes parents do the work for their children. Sensing frustration, they believe it will be easier to do the work than to help their children. Parent tutors need to remember that the objective is to help their children become independent. When frustration becomes too great, quit for a while and come back to it later.

All of these ideas about working with your own children can be summed up easily—make it an enjoyable experience or do not do it.

## TUTORING MORE THAN ONE STUDENT AT A TIME

You might find that you are needed for more than one student. Teaching two or more students at once is not an uncommon assignment. For example, three students might need to have their spelling reinforced. Group work is often more efficient and more fun for the students. Several suggestions are offered in case you find yourself in this situation:

1. Help each student to work to capacity but do not compare one student with another. Public comparison is, of course, humiliating.
2. Keep students on task. If the session drags on and on, change it. Try something different.
3. Find out which students work best together and arrange the seating accordingly. Much of the work in school can be best accomplished when students are paired. That permits them to help each other and usually results in better products.
4. Prepare for differentiated assignments even though the students might have the same difficulty in school. Allow for different standards, different rates for completing an activity, and different activities when appropriate.
5. Be sure to contact your coordinator when you run into management difficulties.

## TEAM TUTORING

Occasionally tutors work as a team. They plan for and tutor students together. Teaming may be desirable for a number of reasons, some of which are:

1. A beginning tutor can work with an experienced tutor in order to get a good start.
2. A tutor leaving the program can work with the replacement to provide a smooth transition for the students.
3. Two tutors want to work together.
4. Two tutors have a good mix of skills or experiences.
5. The regular tutor wants to bring in another for a specified period to supplement the program.
6. Students still receive help even when one tutor is absent. If a tutor is ill or needs to be out of town, the other tutor can continue the program.

While teaming has many advantages, it also has drawbacks. The following suggestions might help you to avoid or at least understand those drawbacks:

1.  Expect to spend more time planning. Teaming requires teamwork. You must know what each of you is going to do.
2.  Tutors have strengths and weaknesses. These need to be acknowledged so that the most efficient plan can be developed. For example, one tutor might claim to be poor at teaching writing skills, but good in working with children on arithmetic. The other tutor might be poor with arithmetic but good at teaching writing.
3.  Plan for continuous evaluation, and make adjustments based upon that evaluation. Do not let annoying or inefficient practices continue. You might find that teaming is only useful for a specific period and not thereafter.
4.  Talk about the work load. A tutor who feels overloaded in a team situation can quickly become dissatisfied.

The general principles of tutoring contained in this book can be applied in many other contexts. Whatever your particular situation, if you are excited about your program and interested in your students, the tutoring experience should be as rewarding for you as for those you tutor.

# Appendices
# Index

# APPENDIX A   Sample Instructional Activities for Tutoring

This section includes a few samples of activities frequently used in tutoring. They are briefly described here to give you an idea of the components of an instructional activity. If you plan to use any of these strategies in your tutoring, be sure to get further information from your coordinator.

## READING BOOKS TO STUDENTS

*Purpose.*   To stimulate interest in reading by reading aloud to students.

*Explanation.*   Many students do not enjoy reading because it is too difficult for them. But they can enjoy literature when they are read to by a mature reader.

*Procedures*
1. Plan some time during every tutoring period for reading to your students.
2. Take at least three library books to the tutoring session. Rehearse your reading of these books so you will be very fluent. Consider the students' interests and attention span in your selection. Let the students choose the book to be read. Be sure to select books you will enjoy too! Your students will be able to tell if you like the story.
3. Introduce the book in a meaningful way such as:
   • telling something interesting you read in the story. Example: The story is about Peter who does not have anything to do. One day he gets a big ball of string, and he does something that gets him into big trouble.
   • asking a question about the title or a picture. Example: The lion's name is King. Do you think that might be a good name for him? Let's read the story to find out.
4. Provide a comfortable situation for reading. Sit near the students so they can see the illustrations and enjoy the story together. Involve the students during the reading when appropriate.
5. Reflect upon what has been read. Find out if your students enjoyed the story. You might discuss a favorite incident, character, or

play a game where you take turns asking each other questions about the story. Make certain that this reflection session is a pleasant one.

## USING STUDENT-DEVELOPED STORIES AS READING MATERIALS

*Purpose.*   To develop reading skills using personally meaningful material.

*Explanation.*   Students can dictate stories to a tutor and express personally meaningful ideas. This material, when used for reading instruction, is highly motivating. Student attention is therefore greatly increased.

*Procedures.*   Check with your coordinator about using student-generated materials. If the coordinator thinks they are appropriate, try some of the following activities:
1.   Discuss with your students an experience common to them.
2.   After the discussion, inform the students that you are going to help them write a story about it.
3.   Let them tell you about the experience. Record exactly what they say. Pay close attention to spelling and write clearly. Read each sentence back. Ask them to read the story to you. Read it with them if desirable.
4.   Ask students to select words from the story they want to learn. Help them make a word bank of those words (see "Ways to Learn New Words" below).
5.   File these stories for rereading and for student use.

## WAYS TO LEARN NEW WORDS

*Purpose.*   To help the student learn the meaning and pronunciation of new words.

*Explanation.*   Mature reading is enhanced when students know a large number of words that they can handle with ease. When this happens the reader can devote attention to meaning.

*Procedures*
1.  Help your students build word banks. Write new words that a student wants to learn on three-by-five cards, one word per card. Print the word neatly on the front of the card. Turn the card over and write a sentence using the word dictated by your student. File these in alphabetical order in a box or envelope for quick retrieval.
2.  Review word cards often. All need not be read, but some type of frequent review is necessary. When students do not know a card in the word bank, let them read the sentence on the back as a clue. If they do not know it after reading the sentence, tell them, let them tell you, and put it back in the bank.
3.  Check with your students' teachers concerning ways to use the word banks. Many teachers have special ways they prefer. Some of them are:
    •  Find all of the action words in the bank.
    •  Find words that you know and build a sentence.
    •  Find words with common endings, such as *cat, fat, mat.*

Keep an eye on your students' enthusiasm for these types of activities. At any sign of boredom or frustration, change the activity.

## USING GAMES TO INCREASE VOCABULARY

*Purpose.*    To help students learn new words through the use of games.

*Explanation.*    If the game format is used, learning new words can become fun.

*Procedures.*    Check with your tutoring coordinator to determine if the use of games with your students is appropriate. If so, make some games and have fun.

1.  Select a game board. You can use one that you have at home. Checkers, Monopoly, and others do just fine. Place a newly learned word on each game square. To play the game, students must first pronounce the word and use it in a sentence. They then can complete their turns according to the regular game rules.
2.  Games rely upon a certain amount of luck and some skill. That makes for winners and losers. Make certain that you are not always the winner (see figure 9 for game-playing tips).
3.  There are short games and long games. Pick a game board that is appropriate for your time with the students.

**FIGURE 9**   Tips for Playing Vocabulary Games with Students

1. When your student's answer is correct, PRAISE HIM OR HER. Say such things as the following:
   a. That's good!
   b. Great! You know a lot of words that begin with ＿＿＿ (beginning letter of correct word).
   c. I liked your description of the dog.

2. If your student hesitates when answering,
   a. Give him or her time to think.
   b. After waiting, give a hint such as:
      • The word has the same beginning sound as ＿＿＿＿＿.
      • The word rhymes with ＿＿＿＿＿.
      • A word that means almost the same thing is ＿＿＿＿＿.

3. If your student gives an incorrect answer, GIVE THE STUDENT SUPPORT in the following way:
   a. Praise him or her for any parts of the answer that may be correct.
   b. Say the correct answer.
   c. Let him or her repeat the correct answer (when appropriate).

4. When *you* are winning most of the games, FIND WAYS FOR YOUR STUDENT TO DO MOST OF THE WINNING. You can help your student win more often by taking a turn only when, for example,
   a. A roll of the die shows a two, four or six.
   b. Your student has taken two turns.
   c. You can spell a word your student has asked you.

---

We suggest that you check with your coordinator before starting this activity because some people might see game-playing as an ineffective use of tutor time. Teachers, parents, and even your students should understand the benefits of game-playing before you employ games in your tutoring program.

## HELPING WITH UNFAMILIAR WORDS

*Purpose.*   To help students unlock words they do not know by sight.

*Explanation.*   Many students have a well-developed set of word attack skills but do not know how to use them. A little direction can help them become independent.

*Procedures*
1.  Try to demonstrate that the best clues for unknown words are often found in the passage being read. We call these *context clues*. Create some examples, such as, "The woman gave the sick child some *medicine*. The sick child did not like it. It tasted bad." If the unknown word was "medicine," the students might get some real help by reading on. So students should be encouraged to read on.
2.  If students can be helped to think about meaning instead of word pronunciation, a correct word might be generated. You might therefore ask, "What word or words would make sense to you in that place in the sentence?" If your students can list a few words that would make sense, then you might encourage picking the one that makes the most sense. Or if the students list "pill," "medicine," and "syrup," you might then ask, "With what sound does the word we are looking for start?" That would eliminate "pill" and "syrup," both of which made as much sense as "medicine."
3.  See if your students can recognize any part of the word. Sometimes that is all that is needed because the known part triggers the entire word.
4.  It might be necessary to look the word up in a dictionary or glossary.

Often the best thing to do is to tell your students the word and get on with the reading. That does not help them gain independence, but there are times when other considerations are more important, for example, finishing the assignment on time.

## READING WITH STUDENTS

*Purpose.*  To enhance comprehension and develop fluency.

*Explanation.*  At times students will encounter material that is too difficult to read alone. Reading with students permits you to help them while they read.

*Procedures (to be done with one student at a time)*
1.  Select an interesting passage. Have your students read it silently.
2.  Proceed to read with your students orally. At first you set the pace and are a bit louder.
3.  Reread the passage orally. Gradually let them set the pace and read louder than you. This may not occur until the second or third reading.

4. You may want to tape record students in the final reading to demonstrate fluency.

## REREADING TO INCREASE COMPREHENSION

*Purpose.* To enhance comprehension and develop fluency.

*Explanation.* Often students get to read something only once and, therefore, see themselves as halting, awkward readers. If opportunities for rereading are provided, students hear themselves read more smoothly and with expression.

*Procedures (to be done with one student at a time)*
1. Select a short, high interest passage (fifty to seventy-five words) that students can read.
2. Always provide for silent reading before any type of oral reading activity.
3. Have students read the passage aloud. Ask them to read it aloud one or two more times.
4. Chart fluency or time needed for reading to demonstrate to the students how they have improved.

## DEVELOPING PERSONAL OUTLINES

*Purpose.* To enhance comprehension by helping students reorganize the ideas of the author.

*Explanation.* Since it is not possible to remember everything one reads, it is essential for students to reorganize the author's ideas in some manner. A personal manner is preferable.

*Procedures*
1. After students have finished reading a passage, ask a personal question such as:
   • What do you think was important in that story?
   • What one idea do you think is worth remembering?
   • What was most interesting to you in that story?
2. Write down any thoughts that come from your students as a result of those questions. When you ask personal questions, you must accept the students' responses.

3. Using the book, ask students to locate supporting details for the ideas generated and record them using the outline format.

1. _____
   Important ideas

   a. _____
      Supporting detail

   b. _____
      Supporting detail

4. Once the personal outline is completed, you can discuss the appropriateness of the ideas that were generated by your students.

This approach is especially useful when working with material where the content needs to be remembered.


## DEVELOPING COMPREHENSION THROUGH DISCUSSION

*Purpose.* To encourage students to discuss ideas from a passage without fear of being wrong.

*Explanation.* Many students are fearful of making mistakes when they are questioned. A discussion format serves to reduce that fear.

*Procedures*
1. Think of ways to help students enter into a discussion with a purpose. For example, after reading an article you might:
   • Discuss the pros and cons of an issue.
   • Discuss what they believe motivated a character to act as he or she did.
   • Discuss the critical events in the story.
   • Discuss how it might have ended differently.
   • Discuss what they think is the author's reason for writing the story.
2. Think of ways of responding to student comments. For example:
   • "Neat idea; I hadn't thought of that."
   • "Let's explore that idea some more."
   • "That's an interesting idea. I thought about it a little differently. I thought . . . ."
3. Remember that in a discussion there does not have to be agreement, and both people can conclude different things. The main

point is that you must develop an approach that does not leave students feeling wrong or criticized.

## USING REAL-LIFE MATERIAL FOR COMPREHENSION

*Purpose.*    To develop reading skills using materials from the students' world.

*Explanation.*    Great motivation can be generated for reading when tutors use materials that appear in a student's life and are personally meaningful.

*Procedures.*    Try some of these ideas:
1.  Have students bring in materials that they need to read, such as newspapers, cereal boxes, applications, or advertisements.
2.  Employ the strategies discussed in this section to use these materials during tutoring (examples: building word banks, reading with, rereading, and seeing important ideas).
3.  Place the materials in folders for future use. As you focus on different comprehension skills, refer to these materials as often as possible to show how the skills are used in real-life situations.

# APPENDIX B  Sample Record-Keeping Form

| Date | Tutoring Activities | Materials |
|------|---------------------|-----------|
|      |                     |           |

# Index

An "F" after a page number indicates that the information is contained in a figure.